MANUAL

Grammar of the Edit

MANUAL

MANUAL

Grammar of the Edit

Roy Thompson

FOCAL PRESS

Focal Press
An imprint of Butterworth-Heinemann
Linacre House, Jordan Hill, Oxford OX2 8DP
225 Wildwood Avenue, Woburn, MA 01801–2041
A division of Reed Educational and Professional Publishing Ltd

℞ A member of the Reed Elsevier plc group

OXFORD   BOSTON   JOHANNESBURG
MELBOURNE   NEW DELHI   SINGAPORE

First published 1993
Reprinted 1994, 1995 (twice), 1996, 1997, 1998

British Library Cataloguing in Publication Data
A catalogue record for this book is available from the
British Library

Library of Congress Cataloging in Publication Data
A catalogue record for this book is available from the
Library of Congress

ISBN 0 240 51340 1

Printed and bound in Great Britain by
Biddles Ltd, Guildford and King's Lynn

Contents

Acknowledgements

I am deeply indebted to the Director, Dr Dietrich Berwanger and staff of the Television Training Centre of Berlin and to the TV Training Course participants from many countries, for whom this short manual was first intended. I am especially indebted to Dr C. Grote, of the TTC, without whose help and encouragement this manual could not have been completed. Also I would like to thank editors and colleagues in the film and TV business, in many lands, whose help I sought.

It is true that any teaching manual can never be complete and the 'Grammar of the Edit' can be no exception to this. I would hope that if the more experienced readers notice any glaring omissions or can suggest improvements they will contact me.

Introduction

Learn your craft, it won't stop you being a genius. (Delacroix)

This manual is about how to make an edit, be it in film or video. It does not matter if the method of joining pictures together is by scissors or laser beam, the problem of learning how to be a good editor remains the same. I have concentrated on where and how an edit is made and not about the machine with which it is done.

It is written mainly for the beginner. I am aware that the experienced editor will be able to disprove many of the practices I describe. Be that as it may, the beginner still has to learn good basic practices from somewhere. So I asked myself the simple question, 'What do I have to learn, to be able to make one good edit between two shots?' The contents of this manual make up the answer.

I have left out programme editing, split edits, pattern editing, pace and so many other important elements, because they are subjects to be dealt with on a different level.

Finally, it is worth repeating the words of a respected editor, now retired, but still passionately keen on the craft. Among many others, it was he who helped me the most with the basic contents. He read the draft and pronounced, 'I wish someone had told me all those things and that simply, when I started, all those years ago'. This manual comes too late for him, but perhaps not for those who are beginning a career in post production.

Roy Thompson, 1992

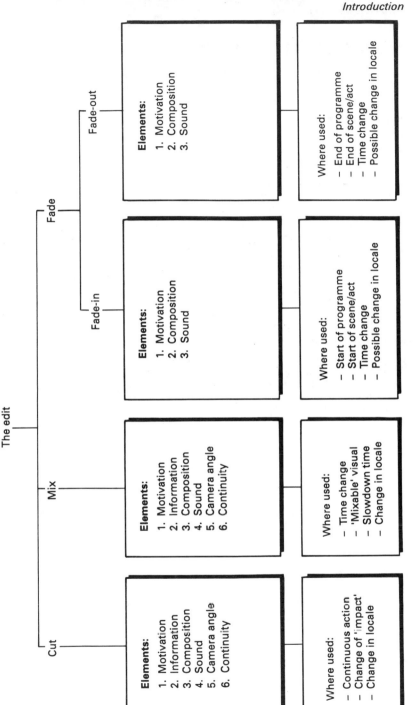

The edit

Fade

Fade-out

Elements:
1. Motivation
2. Composition
3. Sound

Where used:
– End of programme
– End of scene/act
– Time change
– Possible change in locale

Fade-in

Elements:
1. Motivation
2. Composition
3. Sound

Where used:
– Start of programme
– Start of scene/act
– Time change
– Possible change in locale

Mix

Elements:
1. Motivation
2. Information
3. Composition
4. Sound
5. Camera angle
6. Continuity

Where used:
– Time change
– 'Mixable' visual
– Slowdown time
– Change in locale

Cut

Elements:
1. Motivation
2. Information
3. Composition
4. Sound
5. Camera angle
6. Continuity

Where used:
– Continuous action
– Change of 'impact'
– Change in locale

9

Words and Meanings

The words, both nouns and verbs, that we use when describing the editing process have a near precise meaning. These words, born out of the history and practice of film and television, have, over years of constant use, become conventions and have been fully accepted by people who work in the business to mean a certain specific thing, or to be a specific description of an activity.

There are some regional, national and international differences in the names of some operations and shots, but they essentially mean the same thing. In the USA, for example, the 'American (knee) shot' is the same as the 'medium long shot' in the UK, and the shot size does not change in China where it is known by a different word.

Some words are made redundant, or are contrived because of changes in technology. Some have changed because of common usage, in the same way as a language itself changes.

The next few pages are devoted to the most common words used in post production and to their accepted meanings.

Many of these words you will simply become accustomed to. Some you will have to learn by heart. One of the most important groups of words are those describing pictures.

Footage   The raw material with which the editor works. It is a general name given to the processed images, either on video tape that has a recording on it, or on exposed and chemically developed film. It is packaged in different ways.

Spool (noun)   What the footage is wound on to. With film, it arrives packed into round, flat metal or plastic cans. In video, it is packed into plastic boxes of different sizes depending on the format. The spools are within the box. This box is called a cassette.

Spool (verb)   To 'spool' is to wind tape or film from one spool to another, i.e. 'spool on' is to go forwards on the tape or 'spool back' is to go backwards.

Size   Strangely enough, the size of film or video tape is measured in length as well as width. The length of film is described in feet, hence the word 'footage', or in metres, which is more common these days. From the smallest to the largest, film widths are 8 mm, 16 mm, 35 mm and 70 mm.

In video, the sizes are measured in quarters of an inch: 1 quarter inch, half inch, ¾ inch, 1 inch and 2 inch. The length however, is measured in time: half-hour tape, 1 hour tape, etc.

Frame (film)   When you physically examine a piece of exposed and processed movie film, it is fundamentally the same as the film which has been processed after exposure in a normal still cinema. It has the images, either in positive or negative, square sprocket holes down one or both

10

sides, and numbers which identify each individual exposed picture image or frame.

Frame (video)   In video a similar principle applies, except that you cannot see the frames, or the numbers down the edge, and there are no sprocket holes.

Video tape looks like a roll of black plastic tape, dull on one side and shiny on the other. The shiny side is a very thin coat of metal oxide which is responsive to magnetic impulses.

Time code   Because you cannot physically see where you are on a piece of video tape, a special electronic measuring device called a time code reader is used. This tells you exactly where you are. It manifests itself as a series of numbers, shown in pairs, giving the hours, minutes, seconds and frames that have elapsed since the time code started at the beginning of the spool or cassette.

Splicer   In film, the footage is physically cut with a small machine called a splicer and the pictures are 'spliced' together with glue or special sticky tape.

Splice   The word 'splice' is used as a verb when using video and film, e.g. 'splice these two shots together', means cut these two shots together.

Editing (video)   In video, joining the pictures together is done by electronically copying the pictures from one spool onto another using an electronic device called an edit controller. The controller is a simple computer which reads and counts electronic pulses hidden along the edge of the magnetic video tape. It copies then the pictures and sound you select.

Editing (film)   This is the name given to the complete process of putting an entire film together. The operations are carried out with different machines.

Shot   A shot is a series of pictures of an activity or happening or an action. A shot may be either minutes in length or only seconds in length. There are 24 frames for each second in film, but 25 frames per second in video.

Sequence   A number of shots joined together is called a sequence or scene. Sometimes a long scene can contain several sequences.

Take   Each time a shot is filmed or recorded it is called a take. But a shot may have to be repeated a number of times before it is done perfectly, so each time it is made it is given a take number. For example, Scene 4, Shot 16, Take 3.

Good and no good   Because there may be a lot of takes there must be a simple system of noting which ones are usable in the next stage of production, and which are not. The words 'good' and 'no good' are used, and abbreviated as G and NG. Sometimes a NG is referred to as an 'out take'.

Log   Generally, all the shots are written down while shooting. This list is called a log. From this log another list can be made up of the actual shots needed in the scene; this second list is called the edit list or EL. Sometimes the log is called a shot list and sometimes a time code log.

Clapper board   This is the visual record of the shot which is to be filmed. On the clapper board is marked the scene and the take number, together with other information about the shooting. The sound of the board being 'clapped' together is the point at which sound and vision are synchronized together.

   The clapper board is often called a slate. If a board is clapped it indicates that sound and vision are being recorded. If the board is held open it indicates that vision only is being recorded. If the board is shown upside down it shows that it was recorded at the end of the shot and is called an 'end board'. An end board can be also either clapped or mute.

Clip   This is a name given to any piece of film or tape which is taken out of a sequence and used for another purpose.

Colour bars   In video, these are the thick, coloured vertical lines which are recorded first on a tape. They are used to 'line up' the editing machines, so that each time a picture is copied the colour is the same. The colours are, from the left of the screen, white, yellow, cyan, green, magenta, red, blue, and black.

Suite   This is a number of video tape players and recorders needed for editing. Sometimes the room itself is called 'the edit suite'.

Domestic cut off   By 'domestic cut off' is meant an area which is lost when the picture is transmitted and appears on a domestic television set.

   The editor must pay attention to this lost area, as it is possible that the very part of the picture which is of interest to the director may be too close to the edge of the frame to be actually seen in the home. This does not apply directly to cinema, but does if the film is transmitted on TV, which is the case most of the time.

   The editor can do little about domestic cut off, but to accept the fact that it exists and choose shots accordingly.

Cut away (verb)   Editing out of one shot, to another shot which is different in subject matter from the previous one, e.g. 'Cut away from the postman coming through the gate to the dog inside the house, waiting.'

12

Cutaway (noun)   The general name given to any shot which can be used to generate parallel action. "Parallel" action is where two or more activities which may be going on in different places are made to look as though they are happening at the same time, e.g. 'The postman is just coming through the gate, so we need to edit in a cutaway here to see what's waiting for him.'

Shots

Introduction

All shots are subject to four elements which differ in one simple way. The elements either move or they do not move. These elements are:

- the lens

- the camera

- the mounting

- the subject

The lens
There are different kind of lenses with different characteristics. The content of the shot is influenced if the lens is changed or its setting altered.

The camera
The camera can be altered to shoot up or down, which is called a tilt, or to the right or left, which is called a pan.

The mounting
The camera sits on a mounting which can also be moved up or down, elevate or crane up, depress or crane down. It can be moved to the right or left, called a crab, or the mounting can be moved either towards the subject or away from the subject, called a track in or track out. The mounting can be a number of devices ranging from a camera operator's shoulder or a tripod to a fully automated and mechanized camera crane.

The subject
The subject can be a person or persons, a living thing, an animate object or an inanimate object. If the subject is an actor or actors, their movements may be planned in a formal way but, alternatively, there may be no movement at all.

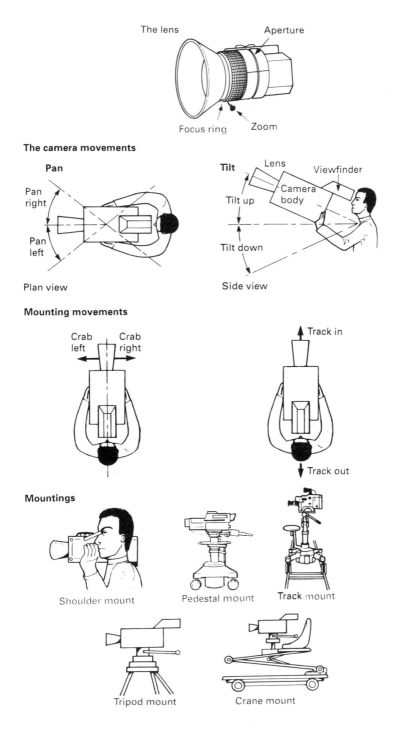

The lens — Aperture

Focus ring — Zoom

The camera movements

Pan

Pan right

Pan left

Plan view

Tilt

Lens — Viewfinder

Tilt up — Camera body

Tilt down

Side view

Mounting movements

Crab left — Crab right

Track in

Track out

Mountings

Shoulder mount

Pedestal mount

Track mount

Tripod mount

Crane mount

15

There are only three types of shots. These are:

- simple shots
- complex shots
- developing shots

The simple shot

A simple shot is a shot containing usually one or more persons, or a shot of an animate or an inanimate object.
    A simple shot has

- *no* lens movement

- *no* camera movement

- *no* mounting movement

- a simple subject movement

There are only a limited number of simple shots of a single person, and an equally limited number of simple shots when a number of people are in the frame.
    The simple shots are described as

- extreme close up (XCU or ECU)
- big close up (BCU)
- close up (CU)
- medium close up (MCU)
- medium shot (MS)
- medium long shot (MLS)
- long shot (LS)
- very long shot (VLS)
- extreme long shot (XLS or ELS)
- two shot (2S)
- over shoulder shot (OSS)

These shot descriptions are part of the basic dialogue which takes place between the editor and other people involved in post production. The correct identification of shots should be part of the editor's basic skills.

1 Extreme close up
2 Big close up
3 Close up
4 Medium close up
5 Medium shot
6 Medium long shot

7 Long shot
8 Very long shot
9 Extremely long shot
10 Two shot
11 Over shoulder shot

17

The complex shot

A complex shot may contain one or more people (or things)

A complex shot has

- a lens movement

- a camera movement

- *no* mounting movement

- a simple subject movement

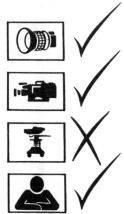

A complex shot has

- *no* mounting movement
- *no* complicated subject movements

Complex shots are:

- a pan
- a tilt
- a pan and tilt
- a lens movement (a focus pull or a zoom)
- a lens movement and pan
- a lens movement and tilt
- a subject movement and pan
- a subject movement and tilt

or any combination of the three elements:

- lens movement
- camera movement
- simple subject movement

The complex shot should have a static start and a static end. The shot is composed or framed in such a way that if the action or subject movement were frozen at any single point, then the resulting picture (frame) would resemble a simple shot.

The developing shot

The developing shot may contain one or more subjects.
   A developing shot has

- a lens movement

- a camera movement

- a camera mounting movement

- a complicated subject movement

The developing shot

The developing shot is perhaps the most difficult shot to make. Like the complex shot it should have a static beginning and a static ending. Also, like the complex shot, if the shot were to be frozen at any point in time, it should ideally resemble a simple shot.

   It differs from the complex shot mainly in the use of the camera mounting and its relationship to the subject movements.

   It is important that the technique of making the shot never interferes with the impact of the visuals. Or, put another way, the good developing shot should never be noticed. Consequently, the good developing shot is complete on its own and often does not need to be edited.

Shot descriptions (simple shots)

1 Extreme close up (XCU or ECU)

The XCU is a detail of a face. For example, one eye, two eyes, the mouth, or perhaps an ear. The detail fills most, if not all, of the entire frame.

The shot is not very common, but within the last few years it has been used in the type of feature films known as 'Spaghetti Westerns'.

The likelihood of meeting an XCU in a dramatic production is not great, as the usefulness of this shot is limited. The shot certainly poses problems in editing a dramatic sequence, as each small movement of a facial expression is magnified to such an extent that it can look silly.

This shot is the least used shot in the range of simple shots.

Sometimes the XCU is used with shots of inanimate objects. For example, the handle of a teacup or the toenail of the foot of an elephant.

In the log, the shot might be marked up as

> XCU teacup handle
or XCU Dumbo's toenail
or XCU Bill's left ear
or XCU Bill's eyes

Examples of the extreme close up (XCU)

2 Big close up (BCU)

The BCU covers the entire face. It is usually composed to show all the features, but does not include the chin line and the top of the head. These framing positions vary depending on the subject. Often with a man, the upper frame edge is on the brow or forehead, but with a woman the shot shows more of the hair line.

The particular problem associated with this shot is the amount of picture that is lost to domestic cut off.

3 Close up (CU)

The CU is a dramatic shot which emphasizes and magnifies facial reactions, or draws particular attention to a specific thing.

The CU is usually a full-face shot and is composed from below the chin and may include the shoulder line. The area of the face covers most of the frame. Subject movement on a close up needs reframing on shot.

It is unlikely that you would be offered a CU with considerable subject movement, as the framing problems during shooting would be too great.

The particular problem encountered with the CU, as with the XCU and the BCU, is the allowance which must be made for domestic cut off. Often a camera operator will frame a small part of the subject's shoulder to ensure that the CU is not affected by 'cut off'.

The problems encountered in editing a CU are few. You should pay attention to any subject movement, and edit out of the shot before the movement alters the shot composition for the worse.

One of the more interesting things about the CU is how the shots of inanimate objects are logged.

Obviously, it is possible to have a CU of a tool. Then a part of that tool might be an even closer shot, a BCU, and then an even smaller part on the BCU, which might become an XCU.

It is an accepted procedure that shots of details of a larger whole can be classified as a CU. The only problem in logging or shot description may arise when there is another shot which is a detail of the last detail.

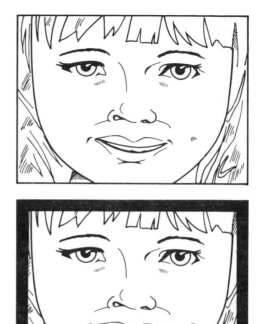

Big close up (BCU)

BCU, showing domestic cut off

Close up (CU)

When the shot contains a part of the human body, for example a hand picking up a telephone, then the description would be, 'CU hand at telephone', where the CU refers to that part of the human body with an inanimate object.

Without the hand in shot, the log might read

    CU telephone
or BCU telephone dial
or XCU dial button No 3

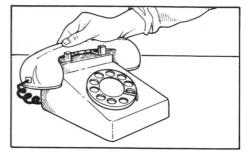

CU hand at telephone

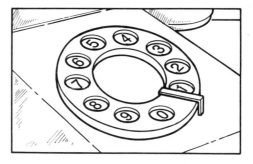

CU telephone

BCU telephone dial

XCU dial button No. 3

4 Medium close up (MCU)

The MCU usually takes one of two forms: either facing the camera, known as 'direct to camera', or 'three-quarter profile'.

In editing for TV, the MCU and the medium shot (MS) are the most commonly used shots. In its first form, direct to camera, the MCU is composed with adequate headroom and is framed above the person's elbow and below the armpit. For example, with a man, it is roughly where the jacket breast pocket might be. With a woman it is just above the elbow joint.

In its second form, the three-quarter profile, the eye which is furthest away from the camera should be approximately on the vertical centre line of the picture. This allows for perfect nose room (looking room).

The nose room is required to ready the viewer's eye to move to the right or left when the picture is edited to another picture of a person. If the nose room is on the left-hand side of the first picture, then it follows that the next picture will have nose room on the right-hand side so that the two people are turned towards each other.

If this doesn't happen, then the two people will appear to be not talking to each other, but to some third person off screen.

Headroom is the distance between the top of the hair and the upper frame edge.

The position of the eyes within the frame depends on the size of the head, whether the subject is a man or a woman, the hair style, and the headroom. Another important factor is whether the subject is wearing a hat or head-dress. All these elements make up a shot and while the descriptions are based on the norm, e.g. 'three-quarter profile, without hat', you should always be aware that variations can and do take place.

MCU, direct to camera

MCU, three-quarter profile

27

5   Medium shot (MS)

The MS is sometimes known as the 'mid shot' or 'waist shot'. It is one of the most commonly used shots and is one of the most flexible in shooting.

The shot is composed from the subject's waist and slightly below. It is never framed higher than the waist because the edge of the frame might be at the same level as the subject's elbow, which would mean a visual confusion if the subject were to raise his or her lower arm.

Headroom in this shot is much greater than previously, as is nose room. The smaller the subject is in the frame, the greater the nose room. The editor must remember on which side of the frame the subject is.

When the subject turns to a three-quarter profile, the same general guide applies. The exception to this is when the subject moves, or is looking at, pointing or gesturing to something. In this case, there will be more nose room. In consequence, the subject may be even more right or left frame.

Certainly, if the subject is to be joined by a second person, then space in the frame will have been provided. This new shot is called a 'medium two shot' (M2S).

Medium shot (MS)

MS, showing greater nose room

Medium two shot (M2S)

29

6 Medium long shot (MLS)

Sometimes known as the 'American (knee) shot', the MLS is generally a movement shot.

If the subject is to move, for instance, at a walking pace, then enough nose room must be provided on the side of the frame towards which the subject will walk. This is especially true when the camera movement is a pan. Then the cameraman will 'lead' the subject rather than follow it, and consequently the subject will, if walking right to left, be framed on the right-hand side of the picture with space on the left-hand side.

If the subject is static, then this does not generally apply.

The framing of a MLS is slightly above or slightly below the knee, but never on the knee. The shot also provides ample headroom and space on each side for arm movement.

Often a MLS can be composed of a group of people and it is especially useful in a complex or developing shot, when there is more camera or camera mounting movement.

7 Long shot (LS)

The LS comprises the entire body and is framed below the feet. Headroom is considerable, as is expected when the subject becomes proportionally smaller within the frame.

The LS is often used as an introductory shot, mainly because the subject is still close enough to be recognized, and far enough away to give some geography to a scene.

The LS is most commonly used when the subject makes a complete movement within the frame, i.e. when there is no need to make a camera movement to follow the subject movement. If the movement is faster, covering swift walking or running for example, then the long shot will be within a complex or developing shot.

Medium long shot (MLS)

MLS, static subject

Long shot (LS)

8 Very long shot (VLS)

The VLS is generally the widest shot ever used which has a single subject still recognizable. But recognition will obviously never be via the face as the subject will be too far away.

In this shot the subject is very small in the frame and consequently headroom is never a problem. When combined with a camera movement, this shot is often used for very fast subject movements, like a car chase. When the subject is static or the movement is small or slow, then the action takes place within the frame.

The shot is very noticeable because of the amount of space around the subject. The position of the subject, frame right or left, top or bottom, is of critical importance for the editor.

This shot is often used for small crowd scenes, and care must be taken when selecting footage where the subject within the crowd does not stray too close to the edge of the frame.

Very long shot (VLS)

VLS, crowd scene

33

9   Extreme long shot (XLS or ELS)

This shot is also called 'the wide angle', 'the wide shot'; even the phrase 'the geography shot' is used.

The subject is so small in the frame that it is totally unrecognizable.

This shot is often used in opening sequences such as a background for titles. 'Westerns' frequently use this shot, where the subject rides from the horizon in XLS to the foreground MS.

The XLS is sometimes provided on a narrow angle, but as this means very complicated lens focusing and often considerable additional shooting problems, it is quite rare. If achieved, it is enthralling, but it takes a great deal of skill and care to edit it.

The normal XLS does give considerable 'geography' to a scene. Depending on the location, it can convey atmosphere and environment. If it is interesting enough it can often be the 'backbone' of the scene.

Again, because of the space around the subject, great care must be taken to remember the subject's position relative to the frame.

Extremely long shot (XLS)

XLS, man on horse

XLS, man in street

35

10 Two shot (2S)

The 2S contains two people, generally either facing camera or each other. The framing depends on a number of factors, whether they are standing or sitting, moving or static, making gestures or not.

In most cases, the normal framing is never closer than a MS, which is still 'tight' if movement or gestures are to be shown. This is redefined as a medium two shot (M2S).

If any arm movements are to be part of the shot, then the framing is more likely to be based on a MLS or wider. The individual subject framing is similar to the normal MS, MLS and LS.

The framing of two people with a closer shot is impossible without one person taking preference on camera. This preference, where one person overlaps the other and is consequently closer to the camera, is called a 'favour'.

When framing more than two people, the shot is known by the number of subjects. For example, a three shot would be a MLS or LS with three people. With more than four people, the framing is approaching a VLS and the shot is referred to either as a 'group shot', or with even more people, in, say, an XLS, as the 'crowd shot'.

Medium two shot (M2S)

2S, favouring the woman

Three shot

11 Over shoulder shot (OSS)

This shot is a development of the 2S. It takes the form of two people, one of which stands with his or her back to the camera.

The normal framing is based on the person in 'favour'; in this case, the favour is given to the person facing the camera. Thus the framing could be of a MCU, with the foreground person (the one nearest the camera) showing only a detail of shoulder, neck and back of his or her head.

As the person in favour relates visually to the foreground (the over shoulder person), the picture composition is very important. Normally the person in favour is framed more to the edge of the frame to allow for the foreground to occupy two or more edges of the frame.

In some cases, the foreground person can be very large, be slightly out of focus, or be standing apparently very close or even a long way away. These factors are due to the position of the camera and the lens angle used.

Some OSSs may have both heads, the one facing and the one back to camera, approximately the same size. Other OSSs may have the foreground head very large. The only recurring element in the OSS is the need to show the shoulder in order to establish where the two people are standing in relation to each other.

When the two people are of different heights, then the camera positions may have changed to a higher or lower position to match the viewpoint of the subject. When this happens, the identification is clarified with the use of the abbreviation HA (high angle) and LA (low angle).

Over shoulder shot (OSS)

OSS, very large foreground

OSS, low angle

OSS, high angle

The Edit

Introduction

The edit is a transition between two shots
It takes one of three forms:

- *The cut.* In the cut, the transition between shot to shot is not perceived by the viewer.
- *The mix.* The mix is a gradual transition from shot to shot by overlapping the images and is perceived by the viewer.
- *The fade.* The fade is a transition, by a gradual change of the image, to a complete black image. It is perceived by the viewer.

Each of these transitions has a completely different meaning and different characteristics, and should be used accordingly.

An edit is built up of a number of elements. How the edit will be depends upon the number of elements used and how they are used, how good or bad, and how obtrusive or unobtrusive.

The six elements of the edit

There are six elements in total, which are as follows:

- **motivation**
- **information**
- **composition**
- **sound**
- **camera angle**
- **continuity**

1 Motivation
There should always be a good reason or motivation to cut, mix or fade. This motivation can be either visual or aural.

In visual terms it could be an action, even of the smallest kind, made by an actor, for example, a body or facial movement.

It could be a sound, like a knock on the door, or a telephone ring or a voice off screen.

The motivation could also be a combination of both vision and sound.

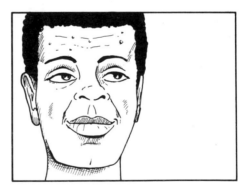

Even a slight smile could be
a motivation to make an edit

2 Information

Information is generally recognized to mean visual information. For the editor, this element is basic to all edits. A new shot means new information. This is simply because if there is no new information in the next shot, then there is little point in cutting to it.

Each shot should, ideally, be a visual treat. In the selection process it must be recognized that however beautiful the shot is, it still should convey visual information different from the last shot.

The more visual information the viewer has and understands, the more informed and involved the viewer becomes.

It is the editor's job to get as much visual information into the programme as he or she can, without patronizing the audience.

This is another reason why the edits must be so smooth that they are unobtrusive.

Cutting these two shots
together gives no new
information

Reaction from a second person is needed

43

3   Shot composition

Over the years, audiences have learned to accept many of the conventions used in programme making.

Although the editor cannot create shot composition, it is part of the editor's job to ensure that a reasonable shot composition exists.

Bad shot composition is a result of bad shooting. It doesn't stop the editing process, but it makes it more difficult.

Standard shot descriptions with their respective composition are dealt with in Chapter 1, but it is worth remembering that not all shots have a standard composition.

It is the editor's job to select the shots with an acceptable composition.

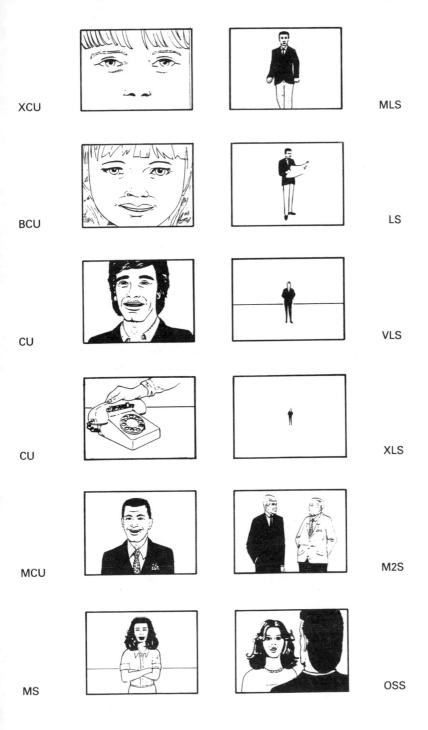

XCU

BCU

CU

CU

MCU

MS

MLS

LS

VLS

XLS

M2S

OSS

45

4 Sound

An important element of the edit can be the sound. Sound is not only more immediate than visuals but also more abstract. The very experienced editors have a saying, 'You don't have to see what you hear.'

Sound can be advanced or delayed to create atmosphere, a heightened sense of tension and many other emotions. For the editor it can be one of the most exciting reasons to make the edit. Sound also can prepare the audience for a change in scene, in location, or even in history.

Lack of the appropriate sound can devalue an edit. For example, consider an office scene where, in the LS, sounds of office machines, typewriters, etc., can be heard. Imagine a cut to a closer shot of a typist without the same sound being heard in the background. That would mean that every single machine had stopped at the instant of the cut to the closer shot.

The audience's attention can also be generated by advanced sound, which is called lapping. For example, it is common to edit the sound four frames in advance of the vision when cutting from an indoor to an outdoor scene.

5 Camera angle

When the director shoots the scene, he or she will have done so from a number of positions (camera angles). From each of these positions the director will have taken a number of shots. The word 'angle' is used to describe these positions of the camera relative to the object or subject.

Imagine the centre of half a spoked wheel. The subject is at the hub. Each spoke could represent a camera axis and the camera positions are on the ends of some of the spokes. The positions vary from one to another, from axis to axis, by a certain distance called 'camera angle'.

The camera angle is one of the most important elements of an edit. The principle is, that each time you cut or mix from one shot to another, the camera should be on a different angle from the previous shot.

For an editor, the difference between the axis should never be greater than 180° and usually less than 45° when shooting the same subject. With experience these figures might be altered considerably.

Office scene with typewriters
and sound

Closer shot of typist.

If the sound stopped
here it would mean
something completely
different.

The accepted meaning of the
term 'camera angle' is the
camera position relative to the
subject – in relation to another
possible camera position to the
same subject. The word camera
'axis' is commonly used

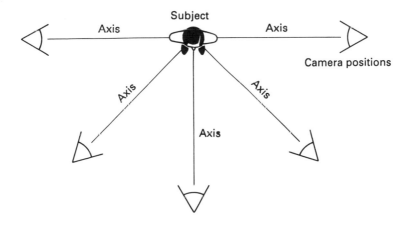

6 Continuity

Each time a new camera angle is being shot (in the same sequence) the actor or presenter will have to perform any movement or action in exactly the same way as he or she did in the previous shot. This, of course, also applies to different 'takes'.

Continuity of content

There should be continuity of content. For example, if the actor has picked up a telephone with his right hand in the first shot, then it is to be expected that the telephone is still in his right hand in any following shot.

Part of the editor's job is to make sure that the continuity is maintained each time an edit is made in a sequence of shots.

Continuity of movement

Continuity also involves direction of movement. If the actor or object is moving right to left on the first shot, then it is to be expected that the actor or subject will move in the same direction in the next shot, unless of course, you see a change in direction actually taking place in the shot.

Continuity of position

Continuity is also important in the position of the actor or subject on the screen. If an actor is on the right-hand side of the screen in the first shot, then he must be on the right-hand side in the next shot also. Unless of course, there has been a stage movement seen on screen to change this.

Continuity of sound

The continuity of sound and its perspective is of critical importance. If the action is happening in the same place in the same 'time', then the sound will continue from one shot to the next one. If there is an aeroplane in the sky in one shot and it is heard, then it needs to be heard in the following shot until the aeroplane is out of distance. Even if the aeroplane is perhaps not seen in the second shot, it does not mean that it should not be heard.

In addition, with shots in the same scene and at the same 'time', there will be a general similarity in background sound. This is known as background ambience, atmosphere, or simply 'atmos'. Atmos must have continuity.

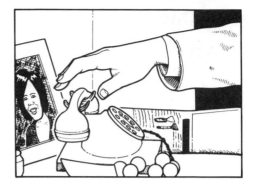

Continuity – the hand that lifts the telephone in the first shot should be the one holding the telephone in the second shot

The Cut

Introduction

The cut is the most commonly used transition. It is an instantaneous change from one shot to another. When it is made correctly it is not consciously noticed.

Of all the three transitions, the cut is what the audience has learned to accept as a form of visual reality.

The cut is used

- where the action is continuous
- where there needs to be a change of 'impact'
- where there is a change of information or locale

The six elements of the cut

A good cut is made up of six elements.

1 Motivation

There should always be a reason to make the cut.

The more skilled an editor, the easier it becomes to find or create a motivation for a cut. Consequently, there develops a greater awareness of exactly where the edit should take place. It also becomes easier to understand how a cut before a motivation – an early cut – works.

A cut after a motivation is called a late cut.

The audience's expectations can be delayed or advanced according to how the editor uses early and late cuts.

2 Information

A new picture should always contain new information.

3 Composition

Each shot should have a reasonable shot composition or framing.

4 Sound

There should ideally be some form of sound continuity or sound development.

5 Camera angle

Each new shot should be on a different camera angle to the last one.

6 Continuity

The movement or action should be both evident and similar in the two shots to be cut together.

General considerations

When the cut becomes visible or noticeable it is called a 'jump cut'. A jump cut acts as a break to the transition from one shot to the next.

As a beginner you should always try to obtain a 'clean cut' and regard the jump cut as an unsatisfactory edit until you know how to use it.

Ideally, each cut should contain all six elements, but not every cut will. A general guide is to include as many elements as possible, depending upon the type of edit.

The editor should know the elements by heart, so that when looking through footage it becomes second routine to check each shot for as many of the six elements as possible.

The Mix

Introduction

The mix is also known as the 'dissolve', the 'lap dissolve', or the 'lap'.

This is the second most commonly used transition from one shot to another. It is made by overlapping the shots, so that near the end of one shot, the beginning of the next shot becomes gradually more visible. As the old shot becomes more faint, the new shot becomes stronger.

This transition is clearly visible.

The centre point of the mix is when each image is equally strong, creating a new image.

A mix must be used with extreme care. The mix is correctly used

- where there is a change in time
- where time needs to be slowed down
- where there is a change in locale
- where there is a strong visual relationship between the outgoing and the incoming images

The six elements of the mix

The mix requires some of the following six elements.

1 Motivation
There should always be a reason to make the mix.

2 Information
The new picture should always contain new visual information.

3 Composition
The two shots to be mixed should have a composition which overlaps easily and avoids visual contradiction.

4 Sound
The sound on both shots should also mix together.

5 Camera angle
The mixed shots should have different camera angles.

6 Time
A mix lasts a minimum of one second and a maximum of three seconds.

With modern machinery there are the possibilities of achieving very fast mix and extremely slow ones. With certain equipment a mix of four frames can be produced easily, or the mix can be as long as the shot itself.

But, if in the centre point of the mix, the images are so pronounced for a long period, then the images appear no longer to be mixed but 'superimposed'. If the mix is short (20 frames or less), it will resemble a visible and badly timed cut.

For the mix to be effective, a one-second maximum mix should be used. If a mix is to be longer, the composition of the pictures must be even more carefully observed. Images confusing for the editor will be more confusing for the audience.

Just before mix

Middle of mix

Just after mix

The Fade

Introduction

The fade is a gradual transition from any image to either a completely black or white screen, or from a black or white screen to any image.
The fade is in two forms:

1 The fade out is the transition of the image to black screen.
2 The fade in (fade up) is the transition from black screen to the image.

The fade in is used

- at the beginning of a programme
- at the beginning of a chapter or scene
- where there is a change in time
- where there is a change in locale

The fade out is used

- at the end of a programme
- at the end of a chapter, scene or act
- where there is a change in time
- where there is a change in locale

The fade out and the fade in are often cut together at the point of 100% black or, rarely, 100% white, thus suggesting the end of one scene and the start of the next. This is also used to separate 'time' and 'place'.

The three elements of the fade

The fade requires three of the six elements.

1 Motivation
There should always be a good reason to make a fade.

2 Composition
The shot ideally should be composed in such a way that the transition to black is gradual overall. That means that there is no great difference between the very lightest part of the picture and the very darkest.

3 Sound
The sound element of the picture should approach some form of climax or ending for the fade out, and the opposite for a fade in.

Fade in from black screen to full image

Fade out from full image to black screen

The Five Types of Edit

Introduction

There are five types of edit:

- action edit
- screen position edit
- form edit
- concept edit
- combined edit

It is important for the editor to be able to recognize all the types of edit and how they are made. The editor must also be able to identify each of the individual 'elements' that are required in an edit.

The action edit

The action edit, sometimes called a movement edit or a continuity edit, is nearly always a cut. It can be made on the simplest gesture or movement; for example, picking up a telephone.

The action edit requires all, or nearly all, of the six elements: motivation, information, shot composition, sound, new camera angle and continuity.

A man is sitting at a desk, the telephone rings, he picks up the phone and answers.

Examine the two shots and identify the six elements.

1 Motivation

When the telephone rings, we know that the man will pick it up and answer it. This would be a good motivation to make the edit.

2 Information

In the LS we are able to see the office, how the man is sitting and what he is doing. The MCU tells us even more about the man. We are now able to see, in greater detail, what he looks like and, more importantly, his reactions to the telephone call. On the MCU we can see some 'body language'. The MCU therefore gives us new information.

3 Shot composition

The shot composition in the LS is reasonably well constructed, even allowing for a plant in the foreground. It gives a general idea of the office and the man is clearly shown to be working at his desk. The MCU is well balanced with correct headroom, although experienced editors may argue that he should have been more screen right, to allow for telephone movement. But the shot composition is acceptable.

4 Sound

There will be the same background sound or atmos in both shots. This atmos might be faint traffic noise outside, or office sounds from an inside source. This will give a sound continuity in both shots.

Action edit, LS

Action edit, MCU

5 Camera angle

In the LS, the camera angle is on a three-quarter profile, almost from the side. In the MCU, the camera is directly in front of the subject. The camera angles are therefore different.

6 Continuity

It is possible to match the arm movement of the subject picking up the telephone on the LS, to the same arm movement on the MCU. In other words, the continuity of body movement exists.

As the edit contains all the six elements, it will be smooth.

As the edit contains all the six elements, it will be unobtrusive.

As the edit contains all the six elements, the visual 'story flow' will not stop.

The screen position edit

This type of edit is sometimes called a directional edit or a placement edit. It can either be a cut or a mix, but is usually a cut if there is no passage of time.

This edit is usually planned in either the pre-production stage or during the shooting stage. It relies on movement or action in the first shot, forcing or directing the eye of the viewer to a new position on the screen.

Example 1

Two walkers stop when they see and point to footsteps of the people they are following.

These two shots will cut together. The camera angle is different and there will be continuity in foot or leg movement. There is now new information and there is sound continuity. The motivation is there – they are actually pointing to it, and the shot composition would work.

The edit contains all six elements. The edit would work and the visual story would not be interrupted.

Screen position edit – Example 1

Example 2

One woman with a gun is threatening another.

Again the cut will work, because of the reasons mentioned in Example 1.

Example 3

A stage. The host of the show is announcing the next act. 'So, Ladies and Gentlemen', he shouts, pointing to the side of the stage, 'please welcome ... the Great Pompisto!!'

Again, the two shots will edit together.

The camera angles are different.

There is new information. We have not seen the Great Pompisto before, and we need to know what he looks like.

The sound would offer great possibilities, cutting either on the applause, or on the words 'please welcome', or after the words if you were to delay the entrance of the Great Pompisto.

There is a motivation to make the cut. Obviously so, the audience have been told they are going to meet him. So, let's meet him!

The shot composition works.

A screen position edit does not always include all six edit elements; however, the greater the number of elements included, the better the screen position edit will be.

Screen position edit – Example 2

Screen position edit – Example 3

The form edit

The form edit is best described as a transition from a shot which has a pronounced shape, colour, dimension or sound, to another shot which has a matching shape, colour, dimension or sound.

With sound as the motivation, the form edit can be a cut, but in most cases it is a mix. This is particularly true when there is a change of location and/or perhaps a change in time.

Example 1

In a hot humid room of the embassy compound, the journalists wait for the relief helicopter to lift them to freedom. On the ceiling a fan rotates. The helicopter arrives.

The edit could be either a cut or a mix. A mix would indicate a greater time difference between the events. The form would be the rotating fan which would match the form of the rotating helicopter blades. The sound could overlap to create either advanced or delayed apprehension.

Example 2

Form edits are often used in advertisements. Here the subject leaning against an upright simulates a company's logo.

There is one big problem which may be encountered with a form edit: that the edit may look too contrived. If used frequently, the form edit becomes predictable.

The beauty of the form edit can be seen when it is done well. And, when it is combined with another type of edit, it can become almost unobtrusive.

Tighten to this

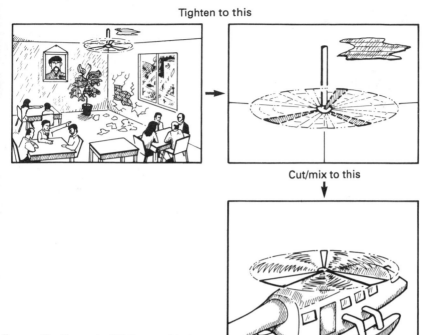

Cut/mix to this

Form edit – Example 1 Helicopter blades

Form edit – Example 2 Woman leans against upright

Kellogg's logo

The concept edit

The concept edit sometimes called dynamic edit or ideas edit, is a purely mental suggestion. Because of the two shots chosen and the point at which the edit is made, the concept edit plants a story in your mind.

The concept edit can cover changes in place, time, people and even in the story itself. It can do so without any visual break.

If the concept edit is well conceived, it can convey moods, make dramatic emphasis and even create abstract ideas. But to do the concept edit well is very difficult. If it is not well planned, the flow of visual information may stop completely.

It is not the elements in the shot that make a concept edit. The effect of what happens when joining the two shots together produces the concept in the viewer's mind.

Here are three examples of some concept edits that have been copied many times over:

- The tear jerker
- The mission impossible
- 'Is there really no hope?'

At its best the concept edit is an original idea, but at worst it becomes a cliché.

If you can't think of a good and original concept edit from the shots available, then it is better to use another type of edit.

The combined edit

The combined edit, without doubt the most difficult of all edit types, is also the most powerful. It is the highest achievement of the editor.

The combined edit combines two or more of the four other edit types: it combines an action (continuity) edit with a screen position edit, and it includes a form edit and even a concept.

Probably one of the best recent examples can be found in the feature film *The French Lieutenant's Woman*. The Director and Editor, Karel Reisz and John Bloom, chose two unusual, but well planned shots, to move the story from an interior modern hotel conservatory setting (in which the actors are rehearsing a film scene) to an exterior woodland setting where the actors are wearing their historical costumes. The cut is made as the actress is rehearsing a 'fall' to the ground and fulfils perfectly all of the six elements of the edit. The continuity requirements of the actresses's fall had to match both shots, making it an action edit. It has requirements of a directional edit, the form was the same in both shots, and finally, the edit creates the idea that takes the viewer from one era to another, a concept edit. Added together, the result is a combined edit.

To achieve a combined edit the editor must be able to recognize the aural and visual potential of each shot as a contribution to the combined edit. Combined edits are carefully planned in both the pre-production and production stages.

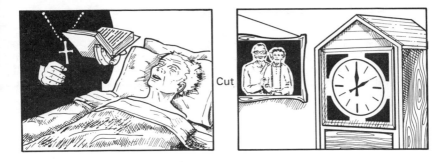

The tear jerker
'. . . et spiritus sanctus. Amen'

The old clock stops ticking

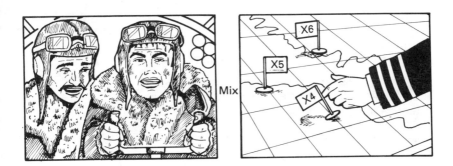

Mission impossible
Navigator to pilot: 'What are the chances
of flight X4 getting back?'

The air marshal's hand
knocks over the X4 flag

65

General Practices

Introduction

The general practices of editing have been changed, developed, refined and handed down from editor to editor over many years. They are based on what editors have found to work. Sometimes the reason why the practice exists is not clear, especially to a beginner. In such a case 'blind acceptance' might be required until growing experience makes the practice more obvious.

The general practices should be regarded as technically binding in nearly all usual circumstances.

There is one practice that all editors claim is of critical importance. It applies to nearly all craft skills and is: 'creativity overrules grammar'. It is also the excuse often given to justify poor craftsmanship.

It is possible to create a new type of edit or develop a new practice, but to do this you must first know the existing edits and practices. But above all, first know and learn the grammar.

The general practices of editing are as follows:

- sound and vision are partners and not rivals
- a new shot should contain new information
- there should be a reason for every edit
- observe the 'line'
- select the appropriate form of edit
- the better the edit, the less it is noticed
- editing is creating

Explanation of the general practices

Sound and vision are partners and not rivals

This seems somewhat obvious, but it is surprising how many editors allow the sound to 'fight' the picture. Sound is a partner in the production and must be edited with the same care and attention to detail as the vision.

The ear and the eye work in unison, supplementing information to each other, so any conflict between the two will cause confusion.

Aural information should extend and expand the message of the visuals. It should give information which enforces and supports the shot.

For example, if a shot shows a car passing a road sign 'Airport', then by adding the appropriate airport sounds, the visual message is enforced and, consequently, more easily understood.

Indeed, certain visuals demand certain sounds. A large bus, for example, demands the sound of a large engine.

In its most simplistic terms, it could be said that an editor should never have a picture on the screen with sounds that do not match. The reason for this is that sound can more quickly create reality than vision. The eye tends to take what it sees factually, whereas sound can stimulate the imagination in a more direct way.

Consequently, 'stimulating the ear to help the eye' is one of the basic tasks of the editor, but if the sound directly contradicts the vision, the result will be confusion and rivalry.

The editor should always remember that sound and vision are tools, that a picture can kill a sound and that sound can kill a picture. Either can dominate, but neither should kill.

Of course there are many examples of the use of 'rivalry and conflict' when editing sound and vision. When done correctly, the results can be very powerful, especially when the sound is linked to the action.

A new shot should contain new information

This general practice is one of the elements of the cut and also one of the elements of the mix. It is almost important enough for it to be called a 'rule'.

The success of a good programme is based on the audience's expectation that there will be a continuous supply of visual information. This supply, if it is correctly delivered, will constantly update and increase the visual information the viewer has of the events of the programme.

There should be a reason for every edit

This convention is linked with *motivation*, one of the six elements of the cut.

If the shot is good and complete in itself, with a beginning, a middle and an end, then it is pointless to cut a section out and replace it – especially if the overall result is not better or more interesting and does not fulfil the expectations of the audience even better than the original shot. In short, do not mutilate a shot. There will be bad consequences before and after if you do!

Also, the reason to make the edit in the first place should be valid under nearly all circumstances. This does not mean that a three-minute monologue from one person to another should not be edited visually. If one person is listening, then that person is likely to make some form of facial or body reaction to what is being said. These reactions should be shown. If, however, the person is talking to himself, without flashbacks and without reference to other shots, and if such a shot is edited only for the reason that the audience should have something else to look at, the very act of editing is likely to break the monologue. If the shot is boring, the fault may lie in the type of shot or the shot composition, or a combination of these things.

Also, merely to cut to another shot to 'up the pace' of the programme is equally suspect. This tendency has developed alarmingly to where a shot lasting more than three seconds is viewed by some producers and directors as being 'boringly long'.

It obviously depends on the production, picture content and viewing habits.

What is acceptable in an action sequence is not acceptable in a love scene.

The reason to make the edit should be worth while. Look for the motivation and the reason, and the edit will then seem 'natural'.

Finally, in deciding the length of a shot, it is essential to give the eyes enough time to read and absorb the visual information.

If in doubt in calculating the time (length) of a shot, then say to yourself (in the example opposite): 'There's the house in the hills – there is smoke coming out of the chimney, the man is walking to the house, it's evening because the sun is setting. Cut!' And that is the length of the shot.

Observe the 'line'

The 'line' is a mental guide for both director and editor as to which side of the subject they are shooting and looking at.

Crossing the line results in a visually contradicting situation for the audience. They are confronted with a different viewpoint of the action and this will change their perception of what is happening.

For example: if a car is travelling from right to left across the screen (diagram 1, camera position A), then the line is the direction of travel. If the next shot is taken from the other side of the line (camera position B), then the car is now appearing to go from left to right, i.e. the opposite way. In reality, the car is actually going the same way as it did before, but on screen it is going in a different direction. Cutting these two shots together, one from side A with one from side B, will break the visual flow and the viewer will be confused and will ask, 'Why is the car now going the opposite way?'

The editor must only select shots from one side of the line unless the line is seen to change, i.e. if the car is seen to change direction on screen.

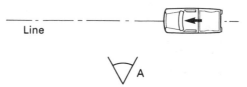

Line

Diagram 1

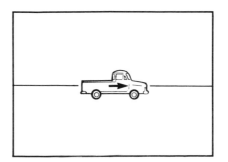

Car as seen from Position A

Car as seen from position B

The line also exists for people. If, as in the next example (diagram 2), the shots are taken from side A, then person 1 is looking to the left and person 2 is looking to the right. The two shots would edit together.

But if one of the shots, say of person 2, was shot from side B, then that person would appear to be also looking left. Clearly, with both persons looking left, they would appear to be talking to some third, but unseen, person off-screen.

Either both shots must come from side A or both from side B, but *never* one from each.

A 'line' exists also for many things. The wind has a line and will blow grass in a certain direction. Machinery has a line. A revolving flywheel, connecting rod and piston have a line. The flywheel shot from one side will be rotating in a clockwise direction, but shot from the other side it would appear to be rotating in an anti-clockwise direction.

What happens in actual reality has no bearing on screen reality. What is happening in real direction has nothing to do with screen direction. Screen reality is an artificial concept and is created by the editor (and director).

In practice, what an editor is doing is reassembling visuals and sound into screen reality.

Select the appropriate form of edit

If a cut is not successful, it does not automatically mean that either a mix or fade will make it successful.

An illegitimate cut is not better than an illegitimate mix.

If two shots will not go together as a cut, then they will certainly not go together as a mix. This is because either:

- the angle is wrong
- or the continuity is wrong
- or there is no new information
- or there is no motivation
- or the shot composition is wrong
- or there is a combination of the above.

There is very little you can do to improve this.

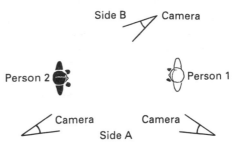

Side B   Camera

Person 2   Person 1

Camera   Camera

Side A

Diagram 2

Shot from side A, person 1

Shot from side A, person 2

Shot from side B, person 2

71

Example

Say the line has been wrongly crossed. Obviously the man or the woman is on the wrong side of the picture. As a cut from one shot to the other there will be the worst type of jump. It will jar the audience visually and it will not flow.

Clearly, the edit as a *cut* would be incorrect.

As a *mix*, the edit would result in total and complete confusion to the viewer. The audience would be quite right to think: 'Why has the woman suddenly changed into a man and the man into a woman?' 'Does this have a special meaning?' 'Has a period of time magically changed her clothing?' 'Perhaps they are the son and daughter of the first pair!'

If an edit is to be a *cut* and it fails as a cut, then the failure might be compounded, even more, as a *mix*.

The better the edit, the less it is noticed

This is the ideal situation. A programme that is well edited will result in the edits not being noticed. If the edits are not seen, the story flows from beginning to end.

Sometimes the edits can be very powerful, merely because of the selection of the shots being edited. But they will still not be 'seen' and as such will help the visual flow. This is the work of a creative editor.

One bad edit often ruins an entire sequence of shots.

It is one of the few areas in programme making where, if the job is done well, it looks as if it need not have been done at all. Or that it could have been done by anybody. That is the hallmark of a good editor.

Editing is creating

It is an old saying that 'rules are made to be broken'. The general practices of editing are no exception to this. Breaking the practices without good reason is foolhardy.

Breaking the practices to achieve a special result is valid under nearly all circumstances. Certainly, when an editor is seeking to achieve these special circumstances, some general working practices at least must be changed. This may be to make bizarre, comic or surreal sequences.

There are very well-known, experienced directors who, with their editors, have produced very creditable results in breaking the fundamentals of editing. Some directors have even used the jump cut to a creative end. But this has always been for a special sequence.

It is usually best to learn the general practices and working practices – the 'grammar' – before trying to break conventions.

But perfect editing grammar is not an end in itself. And if for that reason alone, the greatest working practice of all applies: creativity overrules grammar.

Shot 1

Shot 2. This has crossed the 'line' and will not cut to shot 1

Shots 1 and 2 mixed together. There is now even worse confusion

Working Practices

Introduction

Working practices are good guides, or good tips, for the daily practice of editing.

They have been found to work, even if the reasons why they work are not always known.

A beginner shouldn't break with working practices unless there are very good reasons to do so.

In many cases, the working practices are given in the negative ('don't do . . .'). This is simply the way they have been handed down.

Working practices are likely to change because of fashion, viewing habits and new technology. There are many working practices, but those listed in the following pages are possibly the more important ones.

Finally, there will be cases where an editor has done everything right – the correct type of edit, the correct elements – so that in theory the cut or mix or fade should work. But it doesn't. One of the skills of an editor is to analyse the imperfect edit and find out why it is so. In such a case, it is possible that the answer may not be found in working practices, but in experience. An answer may not even exist. The reason for this is that editing is not a perfect craft. There is always room for creativity and discovery, and that is the beauty of the craft.

Explanation of the working practices

1 Never cut from an incorrectly framed headroom to a correct one (or the other way around)

Reasons

To cut from a correctly framed headroom to an incorrectly framed one will look as if one of the subjects has suddenly altered his or her height.

To cut from an incorrectly framed headroom to a correct one and back again will look as if the first subject is bobbing up and down.

Solutions

The shot is impossible to correct. A few frames of the footage, however, might be usable for cutaways, if it is not too badly framed. If there is not more than one take, the entire shot might have to be rejected and replaced by another, even if the speaker is not seen to be speaking. An over shoulder two shot (OS2S) may be a solution.

Exception

The exception here is when the two shots have the same headroom, even though both are perhaps wrongly framed. Obviously, if the headroom is completely wrong, the shots will look silly.

74

Don't cut this → to this

Or this → to this

But *this* cuts to → this

2   Avoid shots where spurious objects appear to be too close to the subject's head

Reason

This is a question of shot composition which has failed at the shooting stage. If offered such a shot, it is best not to use it if possible.

Solution

There really is no solution to this problem.

Exceptions

You may be able to use this shot if it has so narrow a lens angle that the background is almost completely out of focus. The only other possible use is in a fast montage, where the shot is seen only for a very small period of time.

This is acceptable

But *this is not*

And this *is just silly*

3   Avoid shots where the side frame edge cuts off people
Reason
Again, this is a result of bad framing during the shoot.

Solution
Sometimes the shot can be used, but it depends what comes before and what comes after. It also depends on the duration of the shot.

Opposite are given some examples.

This is bad framing unless it is part of a pan

This is bad framing and is not acceptable

This is acceptable

This is not acceptable

4 Cut matched shots rather than unmatched shots
Reasons
Camera shots with a similar lens angle at a similar distance from the subject have a similar depth of field, provided the shots have a similar shot composition and content.

In diagram 1, two people are standing in a landscape. Camera positions from A and B are at a similar distance from each subject. Both the shots are taken, for example, at a lens angle of 10° and both the shots are framing a medium close-up (MCU). When this is the case, the editor will have backgrounds which are both out of focus to the same extent.

In diagram 2, the camera position has changed. In position B the lens angle is now 40°, but the shot composition remains the same – a MCU.

In this case the background will be in focus. Consequently, the editor would be cutting from a MCU with an 'out of focus' (OOF) background to a MCU with an 'in focus' (IF) background.

There may be other elements in the shot that do not match.

Solution
If a selection of good shots is available, then preference should be given to those with similarity in the quality of the backgrounds.

Exception
Generally, the wider the lens angle used, the more the picture background is in focus. In other words, the depth of field is greater (diagram c).

The exception to the practice is where a wide angle must be used to show a subject movement from foreground to background or the other way around.

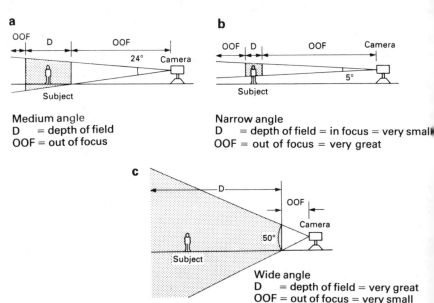

a

OOF D OOF 24° Camera Subject

Medium angle
D   = depth of field
OOF = out of focus

b

OOF D OOF Camera 5° Subject

Narrow angle
D   = depth of field = in focus = very small
OOF = out of focus = very great

c

D OOF Camera 50° Subject

Wide angle
D   = depth of field = very great
OOF = out of focus = very small

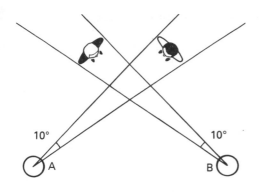

Diagram 1

Shot from A

Shot from B

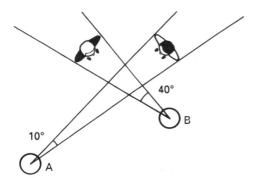

Diagram 2

Shot from A

Shot from B

5   When editing drama dialogue, never edit out a performer's pauses unless requested to do so
Reason
There are some things that can kill a performance, and this is one of them. The performer will have rehearsed the script to achieve a certain emotional impact in the scene. Actors rightly claim that the space between words is just as important as the words. To edit out these spaces (or pauses) in monologue or in dialogue can change, in the worst case, the complete meaning of the scene.

Solutions
Accept the pauses as a guide and use them as a motivation. Accept the pauses as an important integrated element in the dialogue and not just as a moment when someone is not speaking.

Exceptions
The exceptions are all to do with the lack of time.

In news, documentary and current affairs programmes, where the maximum amount of visual and verbal information must be fitted into the minimum amount of time, the editor will obviously need to edit out unnecessary pauses.

6   A reaction shot seems more natural during a phrase or sentence than at the end
Reason
The reason for this is the difference between two distinct situations. In the first, one person may be talking and the second person is listening (and watching) while the first person speaks. In the second situation, one person may be talking and then, when the talking stops, the second person responds to what the first person has said.

The first situation is more interesting, especially when the editor includes shots of the listener reacting as the words are spoken, because it shows communication in action and reaction. It looks much better than the predictable second situation where two persons just talk in turn.

Solution
Look at and listen very carefully to the footage to find a motivation, however small, to insert a cutaway of the listener reacting. If the cutaway is close to the end of the speaker's words, then the cutaway may become the next shot – if it is suitable.

7   Do not be too bound by dialogue when looking for a cut point
Reasons
In dialogue there are two possibilities for cut points: vision and words.

During a two-person dialogue, action and reaction will take place. While one person is talking, the other will be listening and may show facial reactions. These reactions are very important (see the previous working practice).

82

Solution

In the worst case, if no facial reaction is evident, then the director will have shot reaction 'noddies' of the listener as safety shots. 'Noddies' are close shots of the listener simulating a reaction to what is being said. The 'noddies' may be movements of the head, eyebrows, etc. When noddies are cut into the dialogue with a motivation, they can look quite natural.

Noddies are also useful to edit out parts of verbal information. For instance, to reduce the duration of an interview.

The duration of a noddy should be around five seconds, but could be less depending on the circumstances.

Exception

The exception is obviously when the primary shot is a monologue.

8   In a three-person dialogue, never cut from a two shot to another two shot

Reasons

If offered shots of a three-person group which contains 'two shots', then a shot taken from camera position B shows the centre person (person 1) on the right-hand side of the screen. If the editor now cuts to another two shot (2S), from position A, then this shot will show the centre person (person 1) on the left-hand side of the screen, with person 3 on the right-hand side. This is a jump cut.

Solutions

If the shots are available, cut to a single shot of a person instead. For example, cut from a 2S of persons 1 and 2 to a MCU of person 3. Or, conversely, a MCU of person 2 to a 2S of persons 1 and 3.

A long shot could also be used between both two shots.

Exceptions

There are no exceptions to this practice.

84

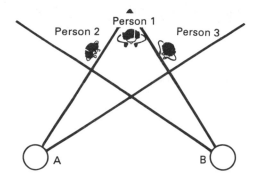

2S from position B (person 1 on right-hand side)

2S from position A (person 1 on left-hand side)

Cutting these two together would be a jump cut

9   On close shots of single characters, the fuller the face the better

Reason

It is better to show the subject's face fully, if emotion or any sort of reaction is to be seen.

Example 1

A man is sitting at a desk. A telephone rings, he picks it up and speaks into it. The two pictures are shot from camera angle A and camera angle B.

Cutting these two shots together will not produce a jump cut, but the subject's face will be almost totally covered by the telephone. In addition, any words he speaks will not be seen to be spoken, and worse still, any reaction or emotion from the subject will be almost entirely hidden.

Therefore, this edit deprives the audience of information. Even though it would make a technically good edit, it breaks the flow of the story.

Example 2

In this example both shots are taken from the same position.

By choosing the close shot of a fuller face (this is a three-quarter profile), the subject's emotions can be more clearly recognized.

Cutting these two shots together runs the risk of a jump cut, because the camera angle of the close up is the same as the camera angle of the long shot.

Therefore, editing these two shots together would tell a better visual story, but in technical terms it is less acceptable because of a possible jump cut.

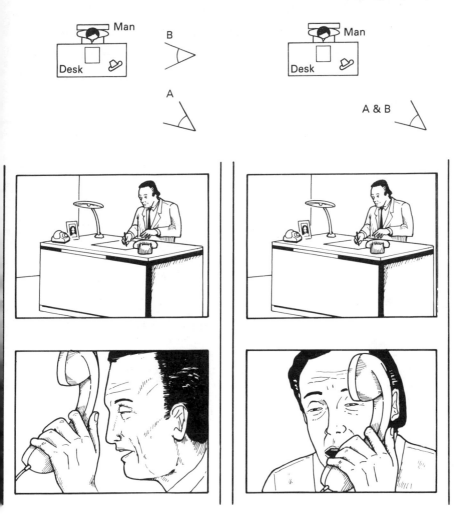

Example 1

Example 2

87

Solution (Example 3)

Here, however, there is no chance of a jump cut.

The two shots will cut well together because of three good reasons.

First, the camera angle is sufficiently different from the long shot, so that the cut will not jump.

Secondly, the subject's face is full face, so that all aural and facial reactions are seen.

Thirdly, matching the movement of the arm in the long shot (from A) to the movement of the hand and forearm in the close shot (from B) is much easier than in the other two previous examples.

Therefore, this combination tells the visual story better and is technically correct.

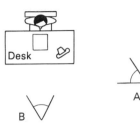

Example 3

Shot A

Shot B

10   With a single character, try to avoid cutting to the same camera angle

Reason

There is a strong chance that a jump cut would result, the reason being that the camera angle has not changed (see 'The six elements of the cut').

In diagram 1, for example, cutting from the long shot (LS) from camera position A into a medium close up (MCU) from position B would present problems. Cutting from a MCU to the LS, however, is less of a problem.

Solution

It would be better to cut to a shot of the MCU from a different camera angle.

In diagram 2, the position of camera B has moved to the right. If a shot from this position were available, the cut would be more interesting and the risk of a jump cut reduced.

In the case where such a shot does not exist, then a cutaway should be used.

This practice is more or less acceptable, depending on whether you cut into a LS or away from a LS.

Exception

The exception to this practice is when cutting two shots together that are *very* dissimilar.

Diagram 1   LS from camera position A
MCU from camera position B

Diagram 2   LS from camera position A
MCU from camera position B

91

11   When cutting the 'rise', try to keep the subject's eyes in frame as long as possible

Reason

The 'rise' is any movement of a subject from a lower to a higher position. For example, the subject sits at a desk (first shot) and then gets up (second shot).

The edit point may be anywhere within the actor's total movement.

Keep the actor's eyes on screen. The subject's eyes are the natural focal point of the viewer's attention. Therefore, the eyes should be in frame as long as possible. This is especially true in close shots.

Solution

A man is seated at a desk. The edit point in Shot 1 will be when his eyes approach the top of the screen, Frame 1c, cutting to Frame 2c in Shot 2. This may seem only a short distance, but actually the subject leans forward before rising. This happens naturally.

If the subject's head is off the screen when the cut is made, Frame 1d, then the edit will appear to be 'late'. If the editor cuts before movement, either on Frame 1a or 1b, so that all the movement is seen on the MLS, Frame 2a or 2b, then the edit is clearly an 'early cut'.

In this solution, 'early' and 'late' cuts are not normally as disturbing as jump cuts.

Exception

One exception to this practice is when the first shot is closer than a MCU. It is almost impossible to cut away from a CU or BCU on a 'rise'. An early cut is almost inevitable.

Shot 1	**Shot 2**

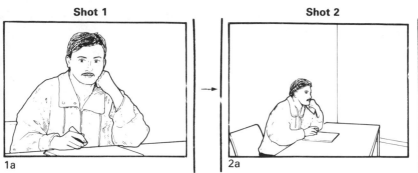

1a 2a

These two shots cut together, but there is no movement, so it is not on the 'rise'.

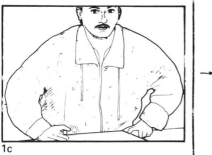 

1b 2b

This would be an 'early cut', because there is no significant upward movement.

1c 2c

This cut would be better. Notice that the eyes are still in the frame in the first shot.

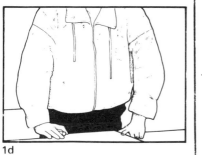 

1d 2d

Now his head has cleared the frame, this would be a 'late cut'.

93

12   When editing in a close up of an action, select a version of the close up where the action is slower

Reason

If the action of the close up (CU) is the same speed as that of the long shot (LS), then the speed of the action, as seen on the close up, seems faster.

For example, the subject is picking up a book in a LS (diagram 1). The CU (diagram 2) shows the hand also picking up the book. The action on the long shot is at normal speed and the book never leaves the frame. But in close shot the book is out of frame very quickly. So, if the close up action is carried out at the same speed, it seems faster.

Solution

The director will usually provide an additional close up with a slightly slower action. The result of editing in the slower version will appear more natural.

Exception

This practice does not apply to shots of moving machinery.

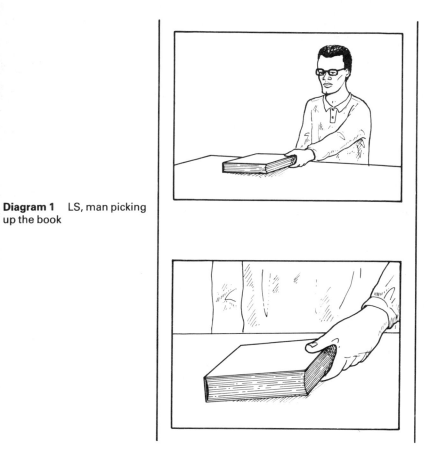

Diagram 1   LS, man picking up the book

Diagram 2   CU, book and hand

13 Prefer a tracking shot to a zoom

Reason

A zoom has a very unnatural effect. It has no change in perspective, so that the horizon (or far distance) and the middle distance will come towards you at the same speed as any objects in the foreground. As our eyes do not zoom, the lens movement will seem unnatural and can break the visual flow.

If you are editing a drama and you are offered a zoom, try to avoid it.

A track on the other hand is a natural movement, will have perspective and is closer to normal vision.

These two sequences of shots show the difference between the zoom and the track.

In documentaries and educational programmes, for example, a shot containing a zoom may be used provided it contains another camera movement at the same time which helps to camouflage the zoom.

Examples

- a tilt with a zoom
- a pan with a zoom
- a crab with a zoom
- an elevation with a zoom, etc.

Exceptions

The only other example of the use of a zoom is when it 'creeps', i.e. when it is so slow that you actually do not realize it is a zoom.

A zoom in TV news is another exception. Obviously a detail of the content is the motivation to make the zoom.

In addition, a zoom in a shot without any discernible background, e.g. a white wall or sky, would be acceptable.

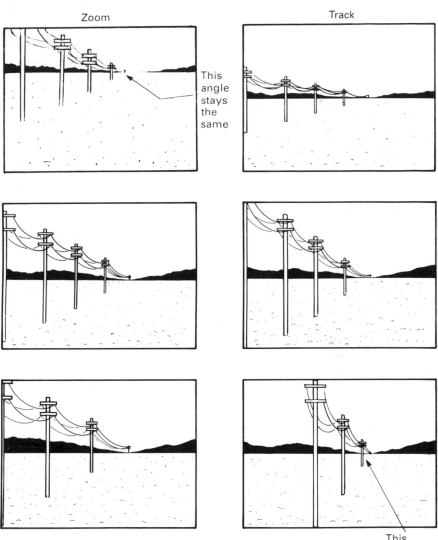

Zoom

Track

This angle stays the same

This angle changes

Poles the same height are equidistant from each other. Therefore, in a zoom the poles enlarge together.

In a track the poles enlarge differently in relation to each other

14   Never use a track out unless it is motivated

Reason

A track out represents the end of a sequence or a scene, and usually precedes either a mix or a cut to another scene or even a fade to black.

Solution

The motivation for the track will usually be included in the shot. In the case where no motivation is evident, or where motivation does not exist in the previous shot, the track out should be treated with extreme caution.

Exceptions

The rare exceptions to this are when a track out must cut to a 'stock shot', or where the track out is the penultimate shot of the production being used partly as a background for credits.

15   When cutting in a pan or a crab, use a version which includes a person or an object which is moving in the same direction as the pan

Reason

The reason is concerned directly with our perception of human scale and movement and its relationship to backgrounds. Take the example of a shot which pans to a door of a building (diagram 1): the scale of the building is not obvious, especially when the top of the building is not seen. Therefore, by selecting a shot which includes a moving person (diagram 2), scale is easier to understand.

Solution

Any person included in the pan must relate to the pan or crab. Consequently, the direction of the walk should be in the same direction as the pan or crab. If there are a number of takes, a shot should be selected where the camera has 'led the subject' (diagram 3), i.e. where there is more frame space before the subject than behind. The pan should of course begin and end with a still frame.

Exceptions

The exceptions to this practice are shots which contain elements that indicate the scale. Another exception would be a shot which is used as a background for credits or titles.

Diagram 1

Diagram 2

Less space here

More space here

Diagram 3

◄—Direction of pan

16 If the objects or subjects are moving within a pan, crab or track, never cut to a static shot of the same objects or subjects (or the opposite way around)

Reason

A cut from or into a camera or pedestal movement will appear as a jump to the eye.

Solution

Take, for example, a subject within a pan (diagram 1) which is moving in the direction of the pan. It is possible to cut to a static shot of the subject, but only when the subject has cleared the frame (diagram 2) for a reasonable time prior to the cut. The shot itself should be static prior to the cut (diagram 3).

Special note

There is much contention among editors as to what an editor attempts when making a cut from or into a pan. Generally, the accepted answer is 'don't', unless the pan is perfect.

There are two reasons for this.

First is the advice: 'Finish or clear the action in the shot before cutting out of the shot.'

Secondly, that the perfect pan is likely to be a complex shot. As such, like a developing shot, it should have a beginning (the initial static frame), a middle (the pan with another movement, tilt or zoom) and an end (the final static frame).

Obviously the correct place for the cut is on the static frame, where the camera is not moving, even though the subject may be.

So, unless the camera stops, and/or the subject stops, and/or the subject is no longer in frame, then it is better not to cut to the same subject, if this subject is stationary.

Exceptions

There are more exceptions to this practice than there are reasons.

Diagram 1
The man is walking right to left

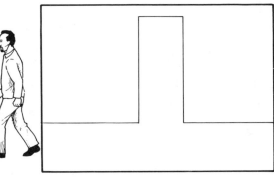

Diagram 2
Let the man clear the frame
before . . .

Diagram 3
. . . cutting to a shot of him
standing still

17 Objects, like people, moving in a direction have a line. Do not cross it or the direction is reversed

Reasons

Refer to: General Practices: Observe the 'line' (p. 68).

In diagram 1, a moving piston is attached to a flywheel which is revolving in a clockwise direction. As seen from camera position A, the shot might look like as shown in diagram 2.

If the line is crossed, i.e. taken from position B (diagram 3), then the wheel appears to be rotating in an anticlockwise direction (diagram 4).

Solution

Select shots from one side of the line only, or use a suitable cutaway between the shots if the line must be crossed.

A CU of part of the machinery held long enough would be suitable.

Obviously, if a crab from one side to the other is used, a jump cut will not appear, but the direction of the wheel is still reversed.

Also bear in mind the application of the previous working practice. If the wheel is moving, do not cut directly to a shot of the wheel stationary.

Exceptions

There are no exceptions to this practice.

102

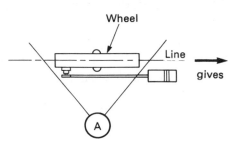

Wheel
Line
gives
A

Diagram 1 Plan

Diagram 2

B
Line
gives

Diagram 3

Diagram 4

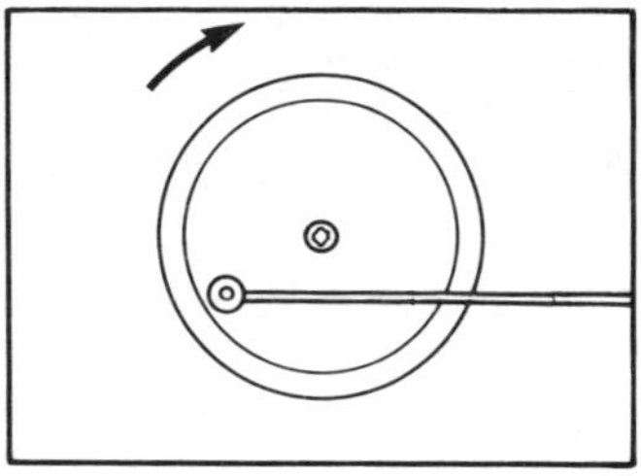

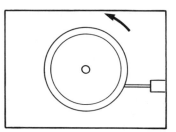

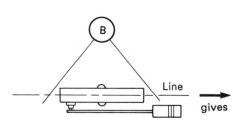

18   Never try to cut an action edit from a two shot to another two shot of the same people

Reasons

An action edit requires near perfect continuity.

It is possible for one actor to maintain perfect continuity of an action. For two, it is almost impossible. For the editor, the task of matching the continuity of two people in an action edit is also impossible. The actors are dealing with their own continuity overall, but the editor is dealing with continuity within fractions of a second.

Solutions

When cutting out of the two shot, cut to a closer shot of one person, some form of reaction shot, or possibly a very long shot. Never attempt to cut to a long shot if the action, and hence the continuity, is recognizable.

Exceptions

The exceptions are where the cut is to a VLS or an XLS.

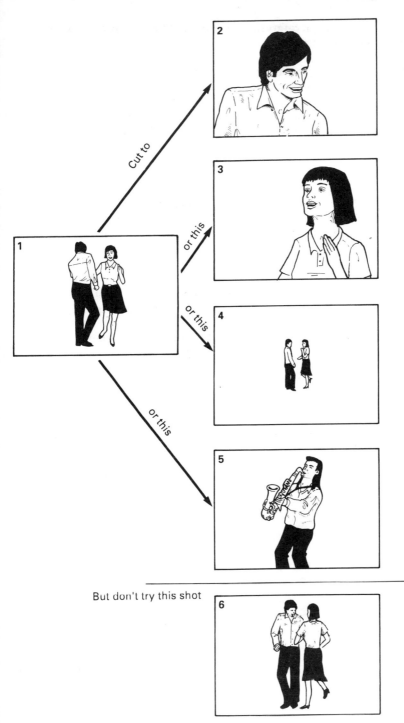

Cut to

or this

or this

or this

But don't try this shot

19 When cutting a telephone conversation together, the head shots should be looking in different directions

Reason

In screen reality, two people who are talking to each other usually look at each other, unless there is a dramatic reason not to.

Solution

The edit is almost a directional edit. Certainly the two speakers in diagram 1 must look in different directions if they are to appear to talk to each other. In addition, the screen position of the speaker and listener should ideally be on opposite sides of the screen (diagram 2).

Exceptions

There may be good dramatic reasons to change this working practice. If one person is shot with his or her back directly towards the camera, then the direction of the other person may be changed.

20 If a character exits frame left, then, for an action edit, the same character should enter the next shot frame right

Reason

This is a very basic practice for any moving thing, object or person. The direction across the screen is constant because that is what the audience expects.

Exceptions

The exceptions to this practice are:

- the direction actually is seen to change on screen
- there is a suggested change of direction on screen followed by a cutaway
- the change of direction is caused by the cutaway (i.e. in the haunted house or murder scene, running in one direction, seeing the ghost, then running the opposite way)

106

Diagram 1   This is acceptable

Diagram 2   But this is better

Exits screen left

Enters screen right

21 Never cut 'point of interest' to 'point of interest'

Reason

Even though the subjects are on the correct side of the screen, the audience will have an additional visual reference, sometimes called the point of interest.

For example, a two shot of a man and woman (diagram 1) shows a painting which is framed centre screen. Cutting to the man (diagram 2) will show the painting screen left. Cutting now to the woman (diagram 3), the point of interest – the painting – has jumped to screen right. Even though the edit is technically correct, the point of interest jumps, and this is visually disturbing.

Solution

Where a point of interest is evident, either keep it in the same area of frame, or select the shots which either eliminate it altogether by selecting closer shots of one or other of the subjects (diagram 4).

Exceptions

An exception to this working practice is where the point of interest is so small as to be negligible, where it is far in the background, or if it is out of focus. Another is where the point of interest is covered, partially or totally, by action.

Diagram 1

Diagram 2

Diagram 3

Diagram 4

22 Give a long shot as soon as possible after a series of close shots

Reason

It is very easy for an audience to forget the exact location of a scene, especially during a fast-moving production.

After a series of MS, MCU and CU shots, particularly those with 'out of focus' backgrounds, it becomes important to re-establish the scene's location.

Solution

Never edit a sequence entirely with close ups unless there is a need to do so.

Even one short LS, showing the relationship of the subjects to each other and to their surroundings, gives a much better understanding of the scene.

Exception

The exception to this practice is where the location or scene is well known to the audience, as in a never ending and popular soap opera production.

After a series of close shots
don't forget to show a long
shot to re-establish a scene

23   On a first entrance of a new character or new subject, edit in a close shot of it

Reasons

The audience will not know the new character or subject, and this may be the first time the character has been seen. The audience needs to absorb a new face and new characteristics.

A long shot will only show the character or subject in relationship to other subjects and to the location, but a new character needs to be closer identified.

Solution

Edit in a closer shot of the character at the earliest opportunity. This also applies if the character is not new but has not been seen for some time. Support the audience by reminding them of events and people.

Exceptions

The obvious exceptions are when the character is an extra or is a 'bit' player.

24   When editing a new scene with new backgrounds, show a long shot at the earliest opportunity

Reasons

The audience needs to know not only what is happening in a new scene, but where it is happening.

Some form of geography is required to establish in the minds of the audience the relationship of subjects to the environment that surrounds them.

In short, some form of wide shot, for example a LS, VLS or XLS, is required. This wide shot should serve a number of purposes:

- to give some geography of the scene, and/or
- to establish the relationship of the character(s) to the surroundings, and/or
- to establish a general impression of movement of the subjects

Exception

The main exception to this practice is when the background to the subject is not in keeping because of style or period.

VLS, butler enters

MCU, 'You rang, sir?'

Give the eye time to 'read' the picture, and give the audience time to see that

... it's a house

... on the plain

... beside the hills

... with a fence

... having smoke coming from the chimney

... trees nearby

... at sunset

113

25   Avoid making an action edit from a long shot of a character to a close up of the same character

Reasons

It is a jump cut to be avoided, unless a shock effect is required or unless the character is recognizable and identifiable in the long shot.

Example

In diagram 1 (plan), a man walks up to a car in VLS. He stops beside the car door and fumbles for his car keys. In two shots, it may look as in (a) and (b).

It will cut together, but it is too much of a jump to the eyes, and the visual reaction may be, 'Who is this new man?', or 'Where have the other man and the car gone?' This edit breaks the visual flow and is therefore unacceptable.

It would be better to use three shots as shown in diagram 2 (plan). The LS to set the scene (i), the MLS at a different angle (ii), and now that he is readily identified, back to the first angle and the CU shot (iii).

The result of having the extra shot in between the two shots is to make the scene flow easier. Now the audience knows where the man is going and what he is doing.

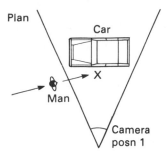

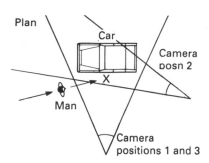

Diagram 1

Diagram 2

115

26 Never cut to black and follow with a cut to picture
Reason
Whatever the intention of the editor, a cut to black, followed by a cut to picture, will seem that a shot is 'missing'.

Solutions
The possible combinations for the end of a sequence or scene and the start of another are either

    cut to next picture
or *mix* to next picture
or *fade* to *black*, *fade up* to picture
or *cut* to *black*, *fade up* to picture
or *fade* to *black*, *cut* to picture

Exceptions
The cut to black and cut to picture is used to break two entire programmes, or two productions or two complete items from each other, or for an effect.

27 At the start of a programme, the sound leads to vision
Reason
The reason for this practice is not clear. Nevertheless, the practice exists. Some editors claim that a picture without sound is dead, but sound without a picture is not.

Obviously the practice depends upon what the sound is and what the opening pictures are in the programme. Provided there are no exceptional circumstances, the sound lead varies between 12 frames and 24 frames. The fade up should match the fade up of the opening shot.

Exceptions
An exception to this practice is in transmission control, where picture is often seen first. Also in advertisements, where the picture is obviously on screen as early as possible for commercial reasons.

28 For the end of a programme, use the end of the music
Reasons
Music, of whatever nature, usually is divided up into different passages, verses or segments and will have a distinct structure. Part of this structure will be an ending or climax. This climax should be used to match the end pictures. As in: General Practices: Sound and vision are partners and not rivals (p. 66), it would be confusing to show the final pictures with the opening musical passage.

Solution
The music should be 'back timed' to find its correct start point relative to the vision sequence. If the timing is correct, the last bars of the musical piece should match the final shots of the sequence. This is especially true

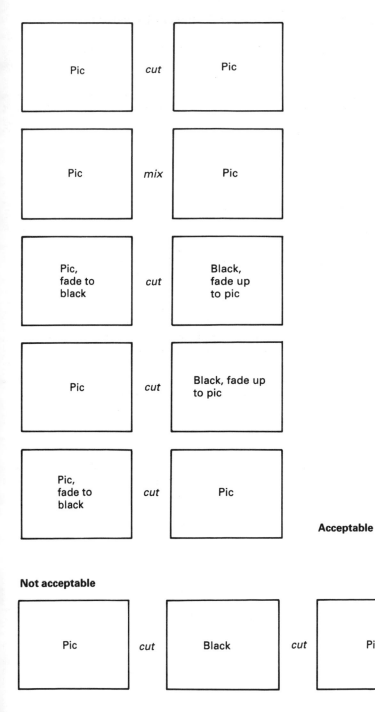

Pic	*cut*	Pic
Pic	*mix*	Pic
Pic, fade to black	*cut*	Black, fade up to pic
Pic	*cut*	Black, fade up to pic
Pic, fade to black	*cut*	Pic

Acceptable

Not acceptable

Pic	*cut*	Black	*cut*	Pic

117

at the end of a programme when the last bar of the music equates with the final caption and the fade to black.

Exception

The main exception to this practice is where the music is faded extremely gradually into or under other sound, dialogue or music which is stronger than the first.